First I win a contest that
makes me a TV star.
Then I get to do some of
the most awesome extreme
sports in the world. And my
two best friends get
to come along for the ride.
How lucky am I?

First published in Great Britain in 2005 by
RISING STARS UK LTD.
76 Farnaby Road, Bromley, BR1 4BH

First published in Australia by Scholastic Australia in 2004.
Text copyright © Philip Kettle, 2004.

A Black Hills book, produced by black dog books

Designed by Blue Boat Design
Cover photo: Blue Boat Design

For more information visit our website at:
www.risingstars-uk.com

British Library Cataloguing in Publication Data

A CIP record for this book is available from the British Library

ISBN 1 905056 45 1

Printed by Bookmarque Ltd, Croydon, Surrey

THE XTREME WORLD OF BILLY KOOL

by Phil Kettle

book:06
mountain biking

RISING ★ STARS

CONTENTS

MOUNTAIN BIKE EQUIPMENT

Chest Guard
If you fall or crash, the chest guard will protect you from rocks and other objects.

Elbow Pads
The elbow pads will also protect you when you fall.

Full-face Helmet
A full-face helmet is needed to prevent damage to any part of the face or skull.

Gloves
Gloves are needed to grip the handlebars as the mountain bike bounces around.

Water Bottle
It's very important to drink plenty of water when mountain biking.

Knee and Shin Pads
Knee and shin pads will protect you when you fall.

Trousers
In rough downhill terrain you need durable trousers to protect your legs.

Mountain Bike Shoes

Mountain bike shoes have good grip to help you keep control of the bike.

Jersey

A light-weight synthetic jersey will allow your skin to breathe in the heat.

A couple of weeks after we'd been skydiving, Sally and I rode our bikes to the park. We were riding at top speed. We wanted to spend as much time as we could on our bikes before we went mountain biking for *The Xtreme World of Billy Kool* on Saturday. But we also didn't want to miss seeing Nathan keep his part of the deal he'd made with Basher Brown.

Nathan had made a bet with

Basher that Basher wouldn't skydive with us. Of course Basher did. Nathan should have realised that if he was brave enough to jump out of a plane, Basher Brown would be as well. So Basher had come onto the show as our special guest star. Well, think about it, if you had the chance to do an extreme sport, you'd be crazy not to take it.

So now, it was Nathan's turn—he had to get back all the cricket balls from the monster's back garden. There were forty-four balls in the monster's back garden and Basher said we had to get all of them. Basher said the deal would not be kept unless every one of the cricket balls was retrieved.

Nathan seemed to think that Sally and I should be helping him even though he had gotten himself into the whole mess in the first place.

We were really into extreme sports, but I don't think the feeling that we got at the thought of going over the monster's fence was anything like the feeling of an extreme sport adrenaline rush. It was more like feeding a shark. You would never be quite sure whether you might all of a sudden become the meal.

'I could throw a bone over the fence and that might distract the monster while you get over the fence and get the balls,' I said.

'Yeah, right,' said Basher. 'It would have to be a huge bone. The monster would eat anything you throw over the fence to him in a second.'

'Yeah,' said Sally.

'Then the monster would look at Nathan and decide that Nathan was dessert and eat him in two seconds.'

4

The cricket balls were getting to be a major problem. There was no way that Basher was ever going to let us forget the bet.

'I hope the people who watch you on TV and think you're heroes never find out how scared you are of a dog,' Basher laughed.

'It's not funny,' said Sally.

'We don't even know what the monster looks like,' said Nathan, who was starting to look really nervous.

'You'll soon find out,' I said.

'Yeah, and the monster might even get to find out what you taste like,' Sally said.

'Billy, you and Sally are my best

friends. You should be helping me,' Nathan said.

'I don't mind helping you,' Sally said. 'But there's no way I'm going over that fence.'

There was no way that I was going either. I had trouble jumping off a bridge even when I knew I wasn't going to get hurt.

'You're both real heroes.' Nathan looked at Sally and me. 'I'm going to get over that fence and I'm going to get every one of those balls ... with or without you.'

'Good,' said Basher. 'We'll have heaps of balls to practise with.' Basher twirled his cricket bat in his hands.

As Basher spoke the monster gave a roar.

Nathan turned and walked away.

'Maybe he's going home. Maybe he's chicken,' said Basher. 'If he doesn't come back then you and Sally have to get the balls.'

There were two things that I knew at that moment. That I was chicken, and that there was no way I was going to get into the garden with the monster.

THE PLAN

We moved away from the fence and
sat on the grass in the middle of the
park.

'What extreme sport are you doing
next?' asked Basher.

'Mountain biking. We're going this
weekend. It'll be unreal,' I said.

'Wish I was coming. Skydiving
was cool. Almost as good as cricket,'
Basher said.

'Look, here comes Nathan,' said
Sally.

Nathan was walking back into the park with a stepladder over his shoulder.

We went over to him. He was looking at us as we walked toward him.

'So, Nathan, how are you going to get over the fence?' Basher asked.

'I'm going to have a look over the fence first and see what the monster looks like,' Nathan said.

The monster must have been able to hear us walking toward the fence. He roared again. We could certainly hear him.

Nathan moved close enough to the fence to rest the ladder against it.

The monster roared even louder as

Nathan started to climb. We stepped a little further back from the fence.

'You can chicken out if you want,' Basher said. He finally seemed to realise how dangerous it was.

'I said I would and I'm going to.' Nathan took another step up the ladder.

The fence started to rock more than I had ever seen it rock before. The monster gave another huge roar. Then it happened. Part of the fence stopped rocking and started to move toward the ground. Nathan and the ladder started to move toward the ground, too.

It was as if it was in slow motion.

We could see what was going to happen. We started to run. Nathan started to fall, and so did the fence.

CRASH!

Nathan hit the ground. The fence hit the ground. There stood the monster—the biggest dog I have ever seen. He was huge and black, with streams of dribble running from the corners of his mouth.

Nathan looked at the dog. He didn't say anything. He just got to his feet and started to run. He only managed to run a few metres before the monster pounced on him and knocked him to the ground.

'The monster is going to eat him!' Sally shouted.

I was too shocked to say anything.
So was Basher.

The monster put both feet on top
of Nathan and pinned him to the
ground.

Just when we thought that
Nathan was about to be eaten, the
monster leant over and started to
lick his face.

We stood still in shock. Then
the monster closed his jaw around
Nathan's wrist. Nathan stood up, his
arm still in the monster's mouth.

I think that Nathan was now far
too scared to scream. The monster
pulled Nathan back through the gap
in the fence and into his backyard.
We started walking toward the gap

in the fence. The type of walk you walk when you might need to turn and run any second.

'The monster's taking him back into his yard for dinner,' whispered Sally.

When we got to the fence and looked through the gap, there was Nathan standing next to the monster. The monster's tail was wagging and in front of the monster on the ground was a pile of cricket balls.

It seemed that the person who was most happy was Basher. That is after Nathan, of course, who was happy that he hadn't turned into the monster's next meal.

Basher got back all forty-four balls that had been hit into the monster's yard.

When we left Basher Park, Basher was still in the middle throwing cricket balls into the air and hitting them as far as he could. The monster was chasing them and bringing them back to him.

Basher Brown might be a lot better at cricket than we are. But that wasn't going to stop us from trying to be better at mountain bike racing than he was. And Nathan, Sally and I had an extreme mountain bike adventure to look forward to at the weekend.

'I reckon I must win the award

for the bravest person in the world,'
Nathan said as we walked home.

Sally and I let him think he was
good. But I bet we were both
thinking the same thing — that
when we went mountain biking on
Saturday we'd be the best.

CAST AND CREW MEETING

For the rest of the week, Nathan, Sally and I spent every spare minute we had riding our bikes. By the end of the week I was taking most of the corners at the park at top speed. I wanted to ride to the studio for the cast and crew meeting, but Mum wouldn't let me. I would have missed the ride in the limo for the extra practise. I really wanted to be good at mountain biking! I wanted to be the best.

When we went to the cast and crew meeting, there was a map pinned up on the wall. It was the mountain bike trail that we'd be taking down the mountain. The camera crew had already gone out to the location and checked out the best positions to shoot from. They had to be in places where they'd get the best footage. But also, it had to be in places where it wasn't likely we'd skid and slam into them.

'You'll also be wearing helmet cams,' the director said. 'It'll be pretty bumpy, so I hope we don't get motion sick watching the video.'

The director said that Shey wanted to go through some of the rules of mountain bike riding. 'Some of them are obvious,' he said, 'like wearing a helmet, but there are others too.'

'What are the rules?' Sally asked.

'Do you want to take over, Shey?' the director asked.

'It's like this,' Shey said. 'Mountain bikers usually share trails with hikers and people riding horses. We've had permission to close off the track as a safety precaution while we're shooting. That way, we'll know that it's only you three on the track. But if you were mountain biking in the real world you'd be sharing a track with people walking, and with horses that can get spooked.

And you'd have to be especially careful when going around bends and blind corners. Also, you're riding in the wild, so you have to be careful not to damage the environment. Make sure that you stay on the path.'

'Alright, people,' the director said. 'That goes for the camera crew as well. And you three, remember tomorrow, pedal with your legs, but ride with your head. The limo will pick you up at 8 o'clock.'

We went home and practised our lines for the morning.

Location Map

1. Starting point at top of hill

2. Rock garden—small rocks that knock your bike around

3. Fallen log to jump over

4. Mud puddle

5. Finish line

6. Sound crew based for monitoring

(5)

(6)

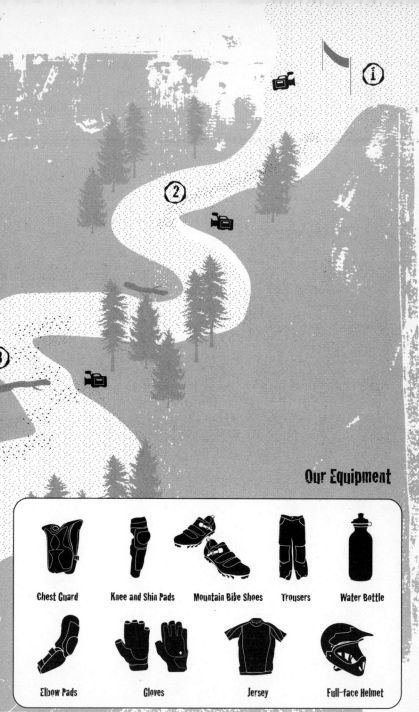

Our Equipment

Chest Guard

Knee and Shin Pads

Mountain Bike Shoes

Trousers

Water Bottle

Elbow Pads

Gloves

Jersey

Full-face Helmet

LIGHT'S, CAMERA, ACTION

BILLY
Hi and welcome to *The Xtreme World of Billy Kool*. My name is Billy Kool and I'm the host of this amazing show. With me are my co-hosts, Sally and Nathan.

SALLY
Hi, Billy and everyone who's watching. Today our extreme sport is mountain biking.

NATHAN
In front of me are the mountain bikes that we're going to race down this huge mountain. I've really been looking forward to this extreme sport.

BILLY
Why mountain biking in particular, Nathan?

NATHAN
Mostly because I'm great when it comes to bike racing.

BILLY
Yeah right, but it takes a lot more than just being able to go fast to be a good extreme mountain bike rider.

SALLY
Yes, that's right Billy. It takes courage, strength, balance and a lot of stamina, which I have got more of than both you and Nathan.

BILLY AND NATHAN
In your dreams.

BILLY
Our safety co-ordinator, Shey, is here to explain more about mountain biking.

SHEY
Hi, everyone. Thanks Billy! Some bikes are designed to ride on roads. But when you want to ride down a mountain at warp speed you need a mountain bike.

NATHAN
What types of mountain bikes are we going to be riding today?

SHEY
These bikes are designed
specifically for downhill
racing. They've got dual-
suspension, which gives
the rider more control
because they're able to
get more traction on the
ground. And if they hit an
obstacle, the suspension
will absorb the impact.

NATHAN
These bikes rock when
you're on rough terrain.

BILLY
We've already had a
practice run on another
track. This downhill track
is totally new to us.

SALLY
Hopefully it was good

enough practice for what
we're about to do.

NATHAN
I was the fastest on the
practice run.

SALLY
Who told you that?

NATHAN
I kept the times on my
watch. That's how I know!

BILLY
I didn't think that we
were having a race then.
I thought that we were
just trying out the bikes.

NATHAN
We were. It was just that
I just tried a lot harder
than you.

SHEY
While Billy, Sally and
Nathan get ready, I am
going to tell you some
more about mountain
biking.

*BILLY, NATHAN and SALLY
put on the safety gear
that is required for
downhill racing.*

SHEY
Mountain biking isn't just
about going fast. Like
any extreme sport, it can
be very dangerous if you
don't know what's ahead
of you. You must wear the
right safety gear. You
also have to keep in mind
that you're sharing the
track with people on foot
and people on horses. It's

also easy to damage the vegetation around you, so you have to stay on the tracks and try not to skid.

SALLY
There are four main types of mountain bike competitions. Cross-country, dual slaloms, trials riding and downhill. Today we are going to do downhill racing. It's one of the fastest competitions and the best to watch.

The camera crew films the slope that Billy, Sally and Nathan are about to go down. It's very steep and twisty.

BILLY
We've got so much gear on,
I reckon we won't get hurt
if we fall off.

SALLY
We're wearing protective
body armour in case we
fall or crash-chest
guards, knee and shin
pads and elbow pads. Of
course we've got full-
face helmets too. Billy
and Nathan certainly look
a lot better with their
helmets on than they do
normally.

BILLY
Thanks.

NATHAN
I like the kneepads and
the elbow and arm pads.

SHEY
Downhill racing is the most spectacular of the extreme mountain bike racing events. This form of racing is reserved for the most fearless of bikers who ride at full speed.

BILLY
That's me.

SALLY
If you think you're that good, you're going first.

BILLY
Alright. I'm up for it. In a downhill race the person who has the fastest time wins. We'll be at the finish line in less than two minutes.

SHEY
Okay, you can be the
spider patrol, Billy.
That's the person who goes
first. They're called that
because they push all the
spider webs and stuff out
of the way for the people
coming behind them.

SALLY
I'm definitely not going
first now.

SHEY
The track is marked out
clearly with different
coloured flags. You have
to get to the bottom as
quickly as you can.

NATHAN
We're wired for sound so
we'll all be able to hear

Billy screaming when he gets covered in cobwebs.

BILLY
Lucky we're wearing full-face helmets.

SALLY
And we'll be able to hear the thump when you hit the ground after you fall off.

SHEY
Okay, Billy, you're up first. I have the stopwatch and I'll keep the times.

Billy pushes his bike to the starting line and checks that his helmet is done up properly.

BILLY
Are you sure that you
don't want to go first,
Sally?

SALLY
No thanks. I'm really
sure that I want you to go
first.

SHEY
Are you ready to go?

BILLY
Yes. My heart's beating
really fast—it must be
adrenaline!

NATHAN
Either that, or maybe it's
just fear.

SHEY
Get set...go!

Billy pushes off and soon picks up speed. His voice comes through clearly.

BILLY
I feel like I'm going a million kilometres per hour. I'm coming into the first corner. I've got to make sure that I put my knee out, move the balance of my body to the back of the bike. I can feel the back wheel starting to slide. The bike is starting to wobble. I'm holding on. I just need to get around the next bend.

NATHAN
Good luck, Billy. You'll need it.

BILLY
I've got around the bend,
the bike is straight
again. I can see the
finish line. It's time to
stand up on the pedals.
Now I've just got to go
as fast as I can. This is
awesome. Here comes the
finish line. Yes, yes,
yes! I made it!

SHEY
Nice one, Billy. Your time
was really good.

BILLY
I'm not too worried about
my time. I'm just glad
that I made it to the
bottom. I thought for
a second I was going to
come off.

NATHAN
Do you need to go to the changing room?

BILLY
No, but you might after your turn.

SHEY
Speaking of which, are you ready to go, Nathan?

NATHAN
I'm ready.

SHEY
Ready, steady, go!

Nathan begins riding.

NATHAN
I've picked up speed so quickly. I feel as if I'm in total control. The bend in the track is coming up.

Oh oh, I think I'm going too fast. I've got my foot out, but the bike's out of control.

BILLY
Watch out for the rock garden at the bend. They nearly got me.

SALLY
Rock garden is slang for small rocks that knock your bike around.

NATHAN
It's wobbling both ways now…I've hit the rocks. I'm in trouble. Aaaaaahhhhhhhhh!

CRASH! Nathan and his bike hit the ground in a big cloud of dust. Nathan is

*hard to see. The dust
settles and Nathan gets to
his feet.*

SHEY
Are you okay, Nathan?

NATHAN
Yeah…I think so. That
really hurt.

BILLY
How was the face plant?

SALLY
Gravity check.

BILLY
Dirt hug.

SHEY
They're all words that
mountain bikers use that
mean crashing.

NATHAN
Yeah, thanks. I never would have figured that out.

BILLY
It just goes to show how careful you have to be doing extreme sports.

SHEY
Yes, Nathan could have really hurt himself so it's lucky he had the right safety gear on!

Nathan gets back on his bike and crosses the finish line even though he knows he has taken too much time for the ride.

NATHAN
That was awesome. Even

if I lost control of the
bike.

SHEY
Well, Sally, it's your
turn.

SALLY
I reckon that I can do
better than both of the
boys.

SHEY
Ready, set, go!

SALLY
This is awesome. I'm
already going at top
speed. I feel in total
control. I love it when I
get this adrenaline rush,
it feels really good.

BILLY
Sally looks like she's

going well…but not as good as me.

SHEY
Sally has taken the first corner. She's one of the best first-time riders that I have ever seen. You're nearly there.

SALLY
Only fifty metres to go to the finish line.

NATHAN
Wow! Sally, you're really good!

Sally crosses the finish line, skids to a stop and takes off her helmet.

SHEY
Good ride, Sally.

SALLY
That was unreal!

BILLY
Sally was really good.
She rode a lot better
than Nathan and me. But of
course if we hadn't showed
her how to ride by going
first, she wouldn't have
been as good.

NATHAN
Yes, you're right, Billy.

SALLY
Whatever.

BILLY
That brings us to the end
of another great show. I
hope you enjoyed it. My
name is Billy Kool. And on
behalf of Nathan and Sally

we look forward to seeing
you next time.

DIRECTOR
That's a take. Well done,
team. That was fantastic!
Great crash, Nathan.

NATHAN
Thanks. I did it for the
camera.

BILLY
Hey, Sally, I want to race
you down the hill again.
Are you up for it?

NATHAN
I want to race you, too.

SALLY
It's not as if you're
going to beat me.

BILLY
There's only one way to
find out.

SALLY
Hurry up. We have to
get home and see what's
happened to the monster.

NATHAN
Basher has probably taken
him home.

THE WRAP UP

Another great show has finished.
I still can't believe that Sally beat
us. Not once, but twice. I reckon
she must have been training for
ages. I can't say too much to her, I
need her to help me with my maths
homework this week.

The monster's owner is a really old
man and he is really pleased that the
monster has made some friends. He
said he isn't going to fix the hole in
the fence. The monster has turned

out to be the biggest, friendliest dog ever, and he really loves cricket. I guess we were a bit sad, because the mystery of the monster was no longer a mystery. But we had found a new friend and a great cricket fielder. Basher reckons the monster is the best fielder he has ever seen.

Dear Billy

I think that I look pretty cool and I'm sure that I would make a great TV star. Please find enclosed a picture of me. From this you can see how cool I am. Do you think I should get an agent?

Jon, a fan

Extreme Information

History

The history of mountain biking is quite recent, though its roots are in the beginnings of bicycle history. In the late 1800s, one of the first bikes appeared. It was called a velocipede, which meant 'fast foot'. Though it quickly became known as a 'boneshaker' as it was made almost entirely of wood and was extremely uncomfortable to ride. Its brakes were its rider's feet.

In 1870, the first bike made entirely out of metal appeared. In the 1890s, a military bike corps of Buffalo Soldiers — black American infantry men — rode over 3000 kilometres from Fort Missoula, across the Rocky Mountains to St Louis. They rode on muddy trails on iron bikes that weighed forty-five kilograms. They were one of the first groups to take bikes off-road and off the beaten track.

Since then, bikes have been adapted to be ridden over rough terrain and very hazardous descents. A boom happened in the 1960s with the development of the *derailleur*, a French word meaning 'de-rail', which made it possible to change gears. This meant that bikes could be ridden on rougher terrain with ease. Mountain biking took off in the United States in the 1970s and soon became a huge extreme sport. It is now an Olympic sport.

Glossary

Air

Space between the tyres and the ground.

BMX

Bike used for stunts and tricks with small tyres.

Bunny hop

A hopping movement on your bike that helps you clear obstacles like logs.

Clean

A perfect ride through a tough section. Also, an obstacle-free trail.

Drop-off

A sudden drop in the trail.

Dualie

A bike with front and rear suspension.

Endo

A crash that sends you flying over the handlebars.

Faceplant

A crash.

Granny gear

The lowest gear you can ride with.

Gravity check

A fall.

Grip

The tyre's traction on the ground.

Rock garden

Small rocks that are easy to skid on.

Spider patrol

The lead rider who clears the cobwebs out of the way.

Equipment

Frame

A mountain bike frame is usually made out of a light-weight but extremely strong material, like aluminium or titanium. It is also lower to the ground than a normal bike and has a longer wheelbase. This lowers the centre of gravity, giving the rider more stability. They are often bigger in diameter and stronger.

Wheels

Mountain bike wheels are smaller in diameter than road bikes, keeping the rider closer to the riding surface. They have aluminium rims with wide tyres for grip and suspension.

Tyres

Mountain bike tyres have larger tread than that on a normal bike. This means that more of the tyre comes into contact with the riding surface, which gives better traction.

Drivetrain

The drivetrain consists of the crank set, the rear sprocket cluster and the chain. The drivetrain makes the bike go forward when the rider pushes the pedals.

Brakes

Most mountain bikes use V-brakes. When the brakes are engaged, the bike stops because of the friction caused when the brake pads grip the wheel rim.

Front and rear derailleurs

The *derailleurs* enable the rider to change

gears. They are operated by shifters which are mounted to the handlebars, so the rider can change gear and still keep a good grip on the handlebars.

Handlebars

Mountain bikes have wide riser handlebars, which keeps the rider more upright, better enabling them to control the bike.

Suspension

Many mountain bikes are equipped with shock-absorbing suspension systems, which make the ride smoother and more comfortable.

PHIL KETTLE

Phil Kettle lives in inner-city Melbourne,
Australia. He has three children, Joel, Ryan and
Shey. Originally from northern Victoria, Phil
grew up on a vineyard. He played football and
cricket and loved any sport where he could kick,
hit or throw something.

These days, Phil likes to go to the Melbourne
Cricket Ground on a winter afternoon and
cheer on his favourite Australian Rules team,
the Richmond Tigers. Phil hopes that one day
he will be able to watch the Tigers win a grand
final—'Even if that means I have to live till
I'm 100.'

THE Xtreme WORLD OF BILLY KOOL

by Phil Kettle

Billy Kool books are available
from most booksellers.
For mail order information
please call Rising Stars on
01933 443862 or visit
www.risingstars-uk.com